Electric Wind
The Story of
William Kamkwamba

Written by Kerrie Shanahan

Flying Start
to Literacy®

Contents

Preface

This is William Kamkwamba.

When William was a boy, he changed his family's lives and the lives of the people in his village. His village did not have electricity, and he worked out a way to make electricity for his village and for his family home.

He now brings wind-powered electricity and water pumps to villages in Africa. This work helps people who don't always have enough food or clean water.

This is William's story.

Can you imagine your life without electricity? When William was growing up, less than 5 per cent of people in Malawi had electricity. Today, only about 11 per cent of people there have electricity.

Chapter 1
Desperate times

When William was a child, he often worked with his dad on his family's farm. They grew a crop called maize, and his family depended on this crop for food.

A village in Malawi

William Kamkwamba
Birthday: 5 August 1987
Home: small village of Wimbe in Malawi, a country in Africa
Family: mother and father and six sisters

A healthy maize crop

Working in the fields with his dad was hard, especially when it was hot, but William didn't complain. He knew how important it was for the maize to grow tall and strong. William's family did not have a lot of money. They lived in a small house and, like almost all people in Malawi, they did not have electricity.

In 2001, Malawi had a terrible drought. There was no rain, and the maize on William's farm was struggling to grow. Months and months went by, and there was still no rain. The maize crop withered and died.

Without any crops, William's family had very little food to eat – there was only enough for one meal a day. William and his sisters were always hungry, and William's parents were worried that they might all starve.

Maize plants in drought

Making porridge from maize

But William and his family did not give up. They planted a new crop and waited for rain. They waited and waited and waited. At long last, it did rain – and the rain helped the new seeds grow. The drought was over.

The next season, William's family had plenty of maize again. Everyone was happy and relieved.

William hoped that things could now return to normal. But something happened that was about to change his life . . .

Chapter 2
Still learning

While working on the family farm, William also went to school. He loved learning and worked hard. When he finished Year Eight, he was accepted into high school. He was very excited!

Students at school in Malawi

An elementary school in Malawi

But William's excitement soon turned to disappointment – he could not go to school. William's parents did not have enough money to pay for him to go.

William was sad, but he understood. His family hardly had enough money to buy food, so they did not have enough to pay William's school fees. They had no choice.

Although William could not go to school, he was determined to keep learning. He was very curious and was always trying to find out how things work – like how a radio makes music, or how the light on a bicycle works.

In his spare time, William visited the library in his village. It was only a small library, but William loved it.

William especially loved the books about science and how things work. He studied the diagrams and drawings in these books for hours. His English wasn't very good, so he would look the words up in a dictionary, or ask the librarian to help him.

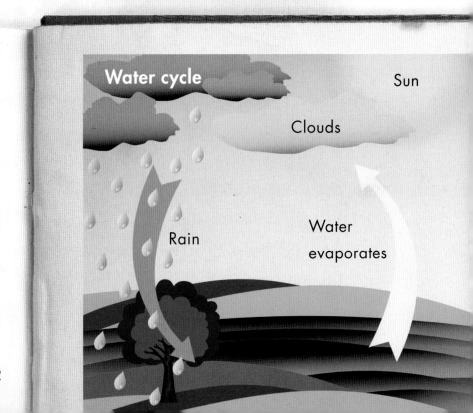

Water cycle

Sun

Clouds

Rain

Water evaporates

The more William read, the more he learnt. And the more William learnt, the more he wondered whether he could find out about something that could somehow help his family.

Could he discover a way to make their lives easier? Could he help his family, so they would never go hungry again?

Chapter 3
William's "crazy" idea

One day, when William was at the library, he came across a book that grabbed his attention. Its title was *Using Energy*, and on the cover it had a picture of a row of tall metal windmills. William read the book.

He learnt that electricity could be made by using wind. He was fascinated.

Electricity would change our lives, William thought.

And this gave him an idea!

William decided that he would build a windmill that made electricity, just like the ones in the book. Then his family could have lights in their home. And William could keep reading at night, instead of going to bed when it got dark.

William also learnt that a windmill could be used to pump water to irrigate their maize.

Wow, thought William. If another drought comes, the windmill could give us the water we need to grow our food!

William could picture in his mind the windmill he wanted to build and how it would work. All he had to do was collect the parts he needed.

But this wasn't as easy as it seemed. William's family had very few belongings, and he certainly couldn't go to the local hardware shop to buy the parts.

So William made many visits to the old junkyard across from the high school. He rummaged through piles of metal, rusty old cars, twisted wire and broken pipes as he looked for the right parts.

Some of the kids from the village laughed at William when they saw him in the junkyard. *"Misala!"* they yelled, which means crazy.

But William didn't care. He was too focused on building his windmill. And so, bit by bit, piece by piece, he collected what he needed – plastic pipe, parts from a broken bicycle, the blade from a tractor fan, pieces of wood, bottle caps, parts from old cars, and other scraps and junk.

Finally, William was ready to build his windmill. He laid out all the parts he had collected from the junkyard, and he began putting them together. He used all of his knowledge and skill to turn the junk into a working windmill.

With the help of his two best friends, he then built a 4.8 metre tower using branches from blue gum trees. As William's tower grew taller, people from the village wondered what he was doing, and they went to his house to find out.

"What is it?" they asked him.

"Electric wind," said William, because there is no word for *windmill* in the Malawi language.

William and his windmill

From the top of the tower, William explained that his machine could make electricity using the power of the wind.

Again, people laughed at William. They didn't believe him! They thought he was crazy.

Chapter 4
Electric wind

Word spread about the "crazy" boy building his machine, and more and more people came to watch him.

When the tower was complete, William hoisted the heavy windmill to the very top, and attached it firmly. The windmill was finished.

William was thrilled but nervous. He looked down at the crowd of people. He knew this was his chance to show everyone that he wasn't crazy and that he really could make electricity. Would his experiment work?

It was time to test his windmill.

William connected a wire to a light socket that held a small light globe. The wind swirled around him. William held his breath.

William's windmill:

- The 4.8 metre tall tower is made from tree trunks.

- The 40 kilogram windmill sits on top of the tower.

Slowly, the blades began to turn. As the wind blew, the blades picked up speed. They began to turn faster and faster as the wind whistled and swirled.

The small light globe that was connected to the windmill flickered. Then it came on, bright and strong!

William's experiment had worked. His windmill was making electricity!

The people in the crowd were amazed. They cheered and clapped, and William proudly smiled his big, wide smile.

William's parents at home

William didn't stop there. Over the next few weeks, he found more wire, enough to reach from the windmill into his house.

He connected the wire to a light globe. William's family gathered around as the light globe lit up their small home. They hugged William, and clapped, and jumped up and down.

The wind kept blowing and William's windmill kept turning. It worked very well and made enough electricity to power four lights and two radios in the family's home. William was even able to charge the mobile phones of some of the people from the village.

Later, the windmill was made taller so that it could catch the wind that blew above the trees. And a second windmill was built that pumped water to the family's maize crops.

In 2006, word began to spread about
the young boy who had made electricity
using the wind. William was interviewed
on the radio and photographed for a
newspaper article.

Soon, William's story of "electric wind" spread
across the Internet and around the world!

Epilogue

In 2007, William Kamkwamba was invited to speak at a Technology, Entertainment and Design (TED) conference. William told his "electric wind" story to a hall full of inventors and scientists.

When he finished, they all stood and clapped. They were amazed at the story of the boy who had used junk to make a windmill that brought electricity to his home.

William at the TED conference in 2007

William's windmill

Success

Testing

Construction

Collecting parts

Idea

Learning

Index